MW01248368

Kenny Chesney

Kenny Chesney: A Journey Through Music and Life

Kenneth Arnold Chesney, better known as Kenny Chesney, was born on March 26, 1968, in Knoxville, Tennessee. Raised in Luttrell, he grew up with deep roots in Southern culture and an appreciation for music that would later define his career. Of English and Irish descent, Chesney is the son of David Chesney, a former elementary school teacher, and Karen Chandler, a hair stylist. He has one younger sister, Jennifer Chandler.

Chesney's passion for music began early. After receiving his first guitar as a Christmas gift, he taught himself to play and developed a love for performing. This interest led him to East Tennessee State University, where he studied advertising and became involved in the ETSU Bluegrass Program. During this time, he recorded a self-released demo album titled Good Old Boy At Heart in 1989, which helped fund the purchase of a new guitar through its sales.

After graduating in 1990, Chesney moved to Nashville, Tennessee, to pursue a career in country music. Performing at local clubs like The Bluebird Cafe and The Turf honed his skills and earned him recognition within the industry. In 1992, Clay Bradley of BMI introduced Chesney to Troy Tomlinson at Opryland Music Group, leading to his first songwriter's contract. A year later, Capricorn Records signed him, marking the beginning of his professional recording career.

Early Career

Chesney's debut album, In My Wildest Dreams , was released in 1994 but failed to achieve significant commercial success due to the closure of Capricorn Records' country division shortly afterward. However, his second album, All I Need to Know (1995), produced two Top 10 hits, "Fall in Love" and the title track, establishing him as a rising star in country music.

By 1997, Chesney had earned his first major award—the Academy of Country Music's New Male Vocalist of the Year—and achieved his first number-one hit with "She's Got It All" from the album I Will Stand . His breakthrough came with Everywhere We Go (1999), which featured two consecutive number-one singles and marked a shift toward the trop rock sound he is now famous for.

Rise to Fame

The release of No Shoes, No Shirt, No Problems in 2002 solidified Chesney's place as a mainstream country artist. The album spawned two chart-topping hits, including "The Good Stuff," which became Billboard's number-one country song of the year. Over the next decade, Chesney continued to dominate the charts with albums such as When the Sun Goes Down (2004), Be as You Are (2005), and Just Who I Am: Poets & Pirates (2007). Each album brought multiple number-one hits and critical acclaim.

Chesney's influence extended beyond music. He collaborated with artists like Jimmy Buffett, Kid Rock, and Reba McEntire, co-wrote songs for Rascal Flatts, and contributed to charity projects. His 2008 documentary The Boys of Fall showcased his storytelling abilities, while his biographical film The Color Orange highlighted his admiration for football legend Condredge Holloway.

Continued Success

Throughout the 2010s, Chesney maintained his status as one of country music's most successful performers. Albums like Hemingway's Whiskey (2010), Welcome to the Fishbowl (2012), and Life on a Rock (2013) demonstrated his versatility, blending traditional country with modern influences. His 2014 album The Big Revival included collaborations with P!NK and Grace Potter, further expanding his audience.

In 2018, Chesney left Sony Music Nashville to sign with Warner Records Nashville, releasing Songs for the Saints , whose proceeds benefited victims of Hurricane Irma. His 2020 album Here and Now debuted at number one on the U.S. Billboard 200, proving his enduring popularity.

Personal Life and Philanthropy

Chesney's personal life has been marked by both triumphs and challenges. In 2005, he married actress Renée Zellweger, though their marriage ended in annulment after four months. Since 2012, he has been in a relationship with Mary Nolan. Known for his commitment to health and fitness, Chesney follows a strict diet and remains active in outdoor activities.

A dedicated philanthropist, Chesney established the Love for Love City foundation to aid those affected by Hurricane Irma in the U.S. Virgin Islands. He also uses his platform to support various causes, donating proceeds from concerts and albums to charitable initiatives.

Legacy

With over 30 million albums sold worldwide, twelve Country Music Association Awards, and numerous other accolades, Kenny Chesney stands as one of the most influential figures in contemporary country music. His ability to connect with fans through relatable lyrics and energetic performances has earned him a loyal following known as the "No Shoes Nation." Whether headlining massive stadium tours or collaborating with fellow musicians, Chesney continues to inspire and entertain audiences across the globe.

As he embarks on new projects, including the upcoming Sun Goes Down Tour with Zac Brown Band in 2024, Kenny Chesney remains a testament to the power of authenticity and perseverance in the world of music.

Later Career Developments

In 2016, Chesney released Cosmic Hallelujah , which featured collaborations with artists like P!NK on "Setting the World on Fire." The album showcased his ability to blend country music with pop influences, further expanding his reach. His live performances continued to draw massive crowds, earning him multiple Billboard Touring Awards for Top Package Tour.

Chesney's 2018 album Songs for the Saints marked a significant moment in his career, as it was inspired by the devastation caused by Hurricane Irma on St. John, U.S. Virgin Islands, where he owns property. All proceeds from the album were donated to his charitable fund, Love for Love City, supporting recovery efforts in the region. This demonstrated his deep connection to the community and commitment to giving back.

The following year, Chesney released Here and Now (2020), which debuted at number one on the U.S. Billboard 200 chart. The album highlighted his enduring appeal, blending introspective lyrics with upbeat tracks that resonated with fans worldwide. Tracks like "Tip of My Tongue" and the title track showcased his versatility as both a songwriter and performer.

In 2024, Chesney is set to release Born , marking another milestone in his illustrious career. Fans eagerly anticipate this new project, which promises to continue the tradition of excellence that has defined his discography.

Tours and Live Performances

Kenny Chesney is renowned not only for his music but also for his electrifying live shows. Over the years, he has headlined some of the most successful tours in country music history, including the Trip Around the Sun Tour (2018), Songs for the Saints Tour (2019), and Here and Now Tour (2022). These tours consistently sold out stadiums across the United States, reinforcing his status as one of the biggest touring acts in the genre.

His co-headlining ventures, such as the Goin' Coastal Tour with Zac Brown Band (2011) and the Brothers of the Sun Tour with Tim McGraw (2012), further cemented his reputation as a collaborative artist who thrives in shared musical experiences. In 2024, Chesney will once again join forces with Zac Brown Band for the Sun Goes Down Tour , promising another unforgettable series of performances.

Cultural Impact and Legacy

Kenny Chesney's influence extends far beyond the realm of country music. He has become synonymous with the laid-back, beach-inspired lifestyle epitomized by his "No Shoes Nation"—a term derived from his hit song "No Shoes, No Shirt, No Problems." This moniker reflects the carefree spirit and communal bond shared by his fans, many of whom have attended his concerts for years.

Through his music, Chesney captures universal themes of love, loss, resilience, and joy, creating an emotional connection with listeners of all ages. Songs like "The Good Stuff," "When I See This Bar," and "Better as a Memory" have become anthems for generations of fans, while his trop rock sound continues to inspire emerging artists.

Beyond his artistic contributions, Chesney's philanthropy underscores his dedication to making a positive impact. Whether through disaster relief efforts or supporting local communities, he uses his platform to uplift others and promote meaningful change.

Looking Ahead

As Kenny Chesney enters the next phase of his career, he remains committed to delivering authentic music and unforgettable live experiences. With upcoming projects like the Sun Goes Down Tour and the release of Born , he continues to push boundaries and explore new creative avenues. For millions of fans around the world, Kenny Chesney represents more than just an entertainer—he embodies a way of life rooted in authenticity, passion, and connection.

Continued Career Growth

In 2016, Kenny Chesney released Cosmic Hallelujah , which featured collaborations with artists like P!NK on "Setting the World on Fire." This track showcased his ability to blend country music with pop sensibilities, expanding his audience further. The album also included "Noise," another single that highlighted his knack for crafting relatable lyrics and catchy melodies.

Chesney's 2018 album Songs for the Saints marked a significant moment in his career as it was inspired by the devastation caused by Hurricane Irma on St. John, U.S. Virgin Islands, where he owns property. Beyond its musical impact, the album served as a tribute to the resilience of the island community. All proceeds from the album were donated to his charitable fund, Love for Love City, underscoring his commitment to giving back.

In 2020, Chesney released Here and Now , which debuted at number one on the U.S. Billboard 200 chart. The album featured the title track and "Tip of My Tongue," a leadoff single that resonated deeply with fans. With this release, Chesney achieved his 16th top-10 album on the Billboard 200, solidifying his status as one of the most consistent performers in the industry.

Recent Projects and Upcoming Releases

Kenny Chesney continues to push creative boundaries with his latest projects. In 2024, he is set to release Born , an eagerly anticipated album that promises to deliver more of the authentic sound fans have come to love. Additionally, he will co-headline the Sun Goes Down Tour with Zac Brown Band, marking yet another milestone in his illustrious touring history.

Personal Life and Interests

Despite his busy schedule, Chesney maintains a disciplined lifestyle. He adheres to a strict diet, avoiding carbohydrates after 5 p.m., and stays active through outdoor activities. His passion for fitness reflects his dedication to maintaining balance amidst his demanding career.

Chesney's spiritual beliefs are rooted in a sense of spirituality rather than organized religion. He has expressed that while he may not agree with all aspects of traditional religious practices, he firmly believes in the transformative power of music and art—a perspective that influences both his songwriting and performances.

Philanthropy and Community Engagement

Philanthropy remains a cornerstone of Chesney's public persona. Following Hurricane Irma in 2017, he demonstrated remarkable generosity by donating the use of his private jet to reunite stranded individuals with their families. Furthermore, he established the Love for Love City foundation to support recovery efforts in the U.S. Virgin Islands, ensuring resources reached those most affected by the disaster.

Through initiatives like Love for Love City, Chesney exemplifies how celebrities can leverage their platforms to drive meaningful change. His actions inspire others to contribute positively to their communities, reinforcing his role as a leader beyond the world of music.

Legacy and Influence

Kenny Chesney's influence extends far beyond his impressive sales figures and accolades. Over three decades, he has built a reputation as a consummate entertainer who connects with audiences through heartfelt storytelling and energetic live performances. Songs like "Young," "The Good Stuff," and "American Kids" have become anthems for generations, capturing universal themes of love, loss, and self-discovery.

His tours remain among the most successful in country music history, drawing massive crowds year after year. Whether headlining solo or collaborating with fellow superstars like Tim McGraw and Zac Brown Band, Chesney consistently delivers unforgettable experiences that leave lasting impressions on fans worldwide.

As he looks toward the future, Kenny Chesney shows no signs of slowing down. With new music, ongoing tours, and continued involvement in charitable endeavors, he continues to shape the landscape of modern country music while inspiring countless others along the way.

Influence in the Music Industry

Kenny Chesney's impact on country music extends beyond his chart-topping hits and record-breaking tours. As one of the most successful touring acts in the genre, he has redefined what it means to be an entertainer. His ability to connect with fans through both his music and live performances has set new standards for engagement and authenticity in the industry.

Chesney is often credited with popularizing the "trop rock" sound within country music—a style characterized by its laid-back, island-inspired vibes. This unique approach not only broadened his audience but also influenced countless artists who followed in his footsteps. Songs like "Beer in Mexico," "Somewhere with You," and "American Kids" have become staples of modern country playlists, showcasing his versatility as a songwriter and performer.

In addition to his musical contributions, Chesney has been a mentor and collaborator to many up-and-coming artists. He has shared the stage with legends such as Jimmy Buffett, Tim McGraw, and Reba McEntire, while also supporting newer talents through co-headlining tours and guest appearances. His willingness to embrace cross-genre collaborations—like his duets with P!NK, Grace Potter, and Dave Matthews—has further solidified his status as a boundary-pushing artist.

Personal Growth and Reflection

Despite his immense success, Kenny Chesney remains grounded in his roots and values. Over the years, he has openly discussed the challenges he faced early in his career, from struggling to break into the Nashville scene to navigating the pressures of fame. These experiences have shaped him into a more introspective artist, evident in albums like Be as You Are (Songs from an Old Blue Chair) and Lucky Old Sun , which explore themes of self-discovery and inner peace.

His relationship with St. John, U.S. Virgin Islands, reflects his appreciation for simplicity and community. After Hurricane Irma devastated the island in 2017, Chesney channeled his grief into action by establishing the Love for Love City foundation. This initiative underscores his commitment to using his platform for good, whether it's rebuilding homes or providing emotional support to those affected by natural disasters.

On a personal level, Chesney continues to prioritize balance in his life. His disciplined lifestyle—including avoiding carbohydrates after 5 p.m.—demonstrates his dedication to maintaining physical and mental well-being amidst a demanding career. Additionally, his spiritual beliefs emphasize the importance of staying connected to one's core values, even when surrounded by external pressures.

Future Endeavors

Looking ahead, Kenny Chesney shows no signs of slowing down. With the release of Born in 2024, fans can expect another chapter in his storied career that blends his signature sounds with fresh perspectives. The album promises to delve deeper into the themes that resonate most with his audience: love, resilience, and the pursuit of happiness.

In addition to his upcoming studio work, Chesney will once again take the stage alongside Zac Brown Band for the Sun Goes Down Tour . Known for their high-energy performances and seamless chemistry, this collaboration is sure to deliver unforgettable moments for fans across the country.

Beyond music, Chesney continues to expand his influence through ventures like No Shoes Radio, his SiriusXM channel dedicated to celebrating the laid-back lifestyle he embodies. By curating playlists that reflect his tastes and sharing stories about the artists featured, he creates a space where listeners feel invited into his world.

Kenny Chesney's legacy as a musician, philanthropist, and cultural icon will endure long after his final concert. Through his music, he has captured the hearts of millions, offering solace, inspiration, and joy to people from all walks of life. His unwavering commitment to authenticity and community has made him a beloved figure in the entertainment industry and beyond.

As he moves forward, Kenny Chesney remains a testament to the power of perseverance, creativity, and kindness. Whether headlining sold-out arenas, supporting charitable causes, or simply enjoying time with loved ones, he continues to inspire others to live life to its fullest potential. For fans worldwide, he will always be synonymous with the carefree spirit and timeless melodies that define the "No Shoes Nation."

Continued Influence in Music and Culture

Kenny Chesney's influence extends beyond his chart-topping hits and sold-out tours. He has become synonymous with the "island-inspired" lifestyle, popularizing what many refer to as the "trop rock" sound—a blend of country, pop, and Caribbean vibes that resonates deeply with fans seeking an escape from everyday life. This unique genre helped him carve out a niche in the country music scene while attracting listeners who may not traditionally follow the genre.

His ability to adapt musically while staying true to his roots has been a hallmark of his career. Albums like Lucky Old Sun (2008) and Hemingway's Whiskey (2010) showcased his willingness to experiment with different sounds, incorporating elements of storytelling, introspection, and even football nostalgia (The Boys of Fall). These projects highlighted Chesney's growth as an artist, proving that he could evolve without alienating his core audience.

Chesney's collaborations have also played a significant role in expanding his reach. Working with artists such as P!NK ("Setting the World on Fire"), Grace Potter (on multiple tracks), and Dave Matthews ("I'm Alive") demonstrated his openness to cross-genre partnerships. Such collaborations introduced him to audiences outside traditional country music circles, reinforcing his status as a versatile entertainer.

The No Shoes Nation Phenomenon

In 2012, Kenny Chesney officially named his fan base "No Shoes Nation," a term derived from his hit song "No Shoes, No Shirt, No Problems." Beyond being just a catchy phrase, this moniker encapsulates the laid-back, carefree spirit that defines his concerts and lifestyle. Fans embraced the identity wholeheartedly, creating a sense of community centered around shared experiences at his live shows.

To further connect with his fans, Chesney launched Live in No Shoes Nation , a live album released in late 2017. It topped the Billboard 200 chart, underscoring the enduring loyalty of his audience. Additionally, the creation of No Shoes Radio —a dedicated SiriusXM channel—provided another platform for Chesney to share his favorite music and stories, deepening the bond between him and his listeners.

Philanthropy and Community Engagement

Philanthropy has always been a central part of Kenny Chesney's public persona. Following Hurricane Irma in 2017, which devastated St. John, U.S. Virgin Islands, where he owns property, Chesney took immediate action. He donated the use of his private jet to reunite stranded individuals with their families and established the Love for Love City foundation to support long-term recovery efforts. By donating all proceeds from his album Songs for the Saints to the fund, he ensured resources reached those most affected by the disaster.

Beyond disaster relief, Chesney uses his platform to promote causes close to his heart. Whether it's supporting local communities or advocating for environmental conservation, he consistently demonstrates his commitment to making a positive impact. His actions inspire others to contribute meaningfully to their own communities, reinforcing his role as more than just a musician but also a leader and advocate.

Recent Developments and Future Plans

In recent years, Kenny Chesney has continued to push boundaries with his music and live performances. His 2020 album Here and Now debuted at number one on the U.S. Billboard 200 chart, marking his 16th top-10 album. Tracks like "Tip of My Tongue" and the title track showcased his ability to craft relatable lyrics that resonate with fans across generations.

Looking ahead, Chesney remains focused on delivering authentic music and unforgettable live experiences. In 2024, he will release Born , an eagerly anticipated studio album that promises to explore new creative avenues. Fans can expect another chapter in his storied career, blending his signature sounds with fresh perspectives.

Additionally, Chesney will co-headline the Sun Goes Down Tour with Zac Brown Band, marking another milestone in his touring history. Known for their high-energy performances and seamless chemistry, this collaboration is sure to deliver memorable moments for fans nationwide.

Personal Life and Reflections

Despite his immense success, Kenny Chesney maintains a grounded perspective on life. He credits much of his inspiration to his experiences growing up in East Tennessee and his love for St. John, U.S. Virgin Islands. Since 2012, he has been in a relationship with Mary Nolan, finding balance amid the demands of his career.

Chesney's spiritual beliefs emphasize the importance of authenticity and connection. While he may not align himself with organized religion, he views spirituality as transformative, often citing how music has the power to change lives. This philosophy permeates his work, both in the studio and on stage.

Legacy and Final Thoughts

Kenny Chesney's legacy as a musician, philanthropist, and cultural icon will endure far beyond his final concert. Through his music, he has captured the hearts of millions, offering solace, inspiration, and joy to people from all walks of life. His unwavering commitment to authenticity and community has made him a beloved figure in the entertainment industry and beyond.

As he moves forward, Kenny Chesney continues to inspire others through his artistry, generosity, and dedication to living life fully. For fans worldwide, he will always be synonymous with the carefree spirit and timeless melodies that define the "No Shoes Nation." Whether headlining sold-out arenas, supporting charitable causes, or simply enjoying time with loved ones, he embodies the essence of authenticity and passion.

Made in United States
Orlando, FL
15 July 2025

62922916R00017